Crime and Justice

THE M. L. SEIDMAN MEMORIAL
TOWN HALL LECTURE SERIES

MEMPHIS STATE UNIVERSITY

The M. L. Seidman Memorial Town Hall Lecture Series was established by P. K. Seidman in memory of his late brother, M. L. Seidman, founder of the firm Seidman and Seidman, Certified Public Accountants.

Publication of this seventh Series of Seidman Lectures was made possible by a gift from Mr. P. K. Seidman to the Memphis State University Press.

The M. L. Seidman Memorial Town Hall Lecture Series

1966-67   *Financial Policies in Transition*
          edited by Dr. Thomas O. Depperschmidt

1967-68   *The USSR in Today's World*
          edited by Dr. Festus Justin Viser

1968-69   *The News Media – A Service and a Force*
          edited by Dr. Festus Justin Viser

1969-70   *Taxation – Dollars and Sense*
          edited by Dr. Festus Justin Viser

1970-71   *The University in Transition*
          edited by Dr. Festus Justin Viser

1971-72   *China's Open Wall*
          edited by Dr. Festus Justin Viser

Crime and Justice

edited by Festus Justin Viser
Professor of Economics
Memphis State University

MEMPHIS STATE UNIVERSITY PRESS   1974

364.973
C868

© COPYRIGHT, 1974
BY MEMPHIS STATE UNIVERSITY PRESS

All Rights Reserved

Library of Congress Cataloging in Publication Data
Main entry under title:

Crime and justice.

   (The M. L. Seidman memorial town hall lecture series)
  1. Crime and criminals—United States—Addresses, essays, lectures. 2. Police corruption—United States—Addresses, essays, lectures. 3. Justice, Administration of—United States—Addresses, essays, lectures. 4. Memphis—Police—Addresses, essays, lectures. I. Viser, Festus Justin, 1920-   ed. II. Title. III. Series.
HV6789.C685   364'.973   74-1064
ISBN 0-87870-019-6

Contents

Preface — ix

Lecture One — 1
"Crime, Hypocrisy, and the Just Society"
by Ramsey Clark

Lecture Two — 11
"Can the Universal Pervasiveness of Police Corruption be Obviated?"
by Whitman Knapp

Lecture Three — 23
"The Search for Interracial Justice"
by Roy Wilkins

Lecture Four — 37
"The Memphis Police Department"
by Jay Hubbard

Coordinating Committee

FESTUS J. VISER, Director
   Professor of Economics
   Memphis State University

FRANK R. AHLGREN
   Retired Editor
   Memphis Commercial Appeal

JERRY N. BOONE
   Vice President for Academic Affairs
   Memphis State University

FRED P. COOK
   Vice President and Station Manager
   WREC AM-FM Radio Station

DENNIS R. HENDRIX
   President
   United Foods, Inc.

MORRIE A. MOSS
   Financial Consultant
   Moss Enterprises, Inc.

MRS. ROLAND H. MYERS
   Hostess, "Challenge to Read"
   WREC Radio

ABE PLOUGH
   Chairman of the Board
   Plough, Inc.

P. K. SEIDMAN
   Partner
   Seidman and Seidman CPA

PHINEAS J. SPARER
   Professor Emeritus
   College of Medicine
   University of Tennessee

Crime and Justice

Preface

The decade of the sixties was characterized by a surging increase in crime. The annual incidence of violent crimes rose from 160 per 100,000 inhabitants to 393 per 100,000 inhabitants for the United States as a whole. Murder increased by 70% throughout the decade, rape by 113% and robbery by a whopping 212%. Even during the first three and one half years of the Nixon Administration, bringing us into the 1970's, major crimes increased by more than 30%.

Justice proved to be an unsure, much debated concept. It is overwhelmingly true that the largest portion of crimes continues to be committed by persons who have been previously confined in penal institutions. Our system of justice is producing more criminals than it is reforming individuals for honest productive lives. Juvenile reform institutions do not work effectively in spite of a cost that exceeds psychotherapeutic institutions or even high cost institutions of higher learning. The whole concept of justice remains hazy in our thinking—we cannot agree on its basic meaning much less its important policy implications.

Then there is the crime record of Memphis. The annual incidence of violent crime has been rising faster than the national average. In fact Memphis finds itself in the category of having the highest incidence of crime for a city of its size in the United States.

These are some of the considerations that led the Coordinating Committee of the M. L. Seidman Memorial Town Hall Lectures to select *Crime and Justice* as the theme for its 1972–73 series. The committee thought that a useful purpose would be served by bringing together several recognized authorities who might have significant things to say about the problem of crime and about the accompanying problem of justice.

The task of selecting spokesmen in the general area of the topic did not prove to be easy. In the first place, four speeches were selected instead of the usual three. This permitted wide coverage and allowed one of the speakers to represent the local Memphis situation.

The Committee wanted well-known authoritative spokesmen as speakers, experienced in the general area of crime and justice or in areas peripheral to it. Yet at the same time it wanted people who would have an original contribution to make.

Very early in the selection process Ramsey Clark was chosen. It was felt that his years as United States Attorney General under President Lyndon B. Johnson plus his daring to stand by his opinion no matter how unique it was eminently qualified him. Also eminently qualified was Judge Whitman Knapp who at the time had just finished his searching look into the question of corruption in the New York City Police Department and who had just been appointed Federal District Judge. Similarly it was felt that Roy Wilkins would have a significant contribution to make after his many years as Executive Director of the National Association for the Advancement of Colored People.

Memphis has in its civil administration a position entitled Director of the Memphis Police Department. This position at the time of the selection of the roster of speakers had just been filled. General Jay Hubbard, as retiring Brigadier General in the Marine Corps, had been selected for the post. The Committee felt that by the spring of 1973, the time of the lectures (the selection was made in the summer of 1972), General Hubbard would be in a unique position to present the story of crime and justice as seen by an objective observer from the vantage point of Memphis. Hence the fourth lecturer was added to the other three.

The best laid plans of mice and of men go astray. This year represented the first lecture cancellation in the history of the series. Mr. Ramsey Clark became entangled in a trial case in San Francisco and he could not extricate himself to deliver his lecture on March 22. He sent his father, the distinguished Justice Tom Clark, as a last minute substitution. In addition Mr. Ramsey Clark submitted an article to be used in this publication in place of his lecture. The article is about the length of the lecture and has been printed in the position that the lecture would otherwise have occupied.

Mr. Clark was born in Dallas, Texas, in 1927. He attended public school there and in Los Angeles, California, and Washington, D. C. In June of 1949 he took a B.A. Degree from the University of Texas. He also holds a M.A. Degree in American History and a J.D. Degree, both from the University of Chicago.

He practiced law in Dallas from 1951 to 1961. He served as United States Assistant Attorney General under President John F. Kennedy. In January of 1965 President Lyndon B. Johnson nominated him Deputy Attorney General and in February of 1967, Attorney General. In July of 1969 he joined the law firm of Paul, Weiss, Rifkind, Wharton and Garrison.

Judge Knapp was born in New York City in 1909.

He took his B.A. Degree from Yale in 1931 and graduated from the Harvard Law School three years later. While at Harvard he served as Editor of the *Harvard Law Review*. He was admitted to the bar in 1935 and began the practice of law in New York City.

From 1937 to 1941 he was Deputy Assistant District Attorney on the staff of Thomas E. Dewey. Then from 1942 to 1950 he was Assistant District Attorney on the staff of Frank S. Hogan. For the next 12 years, he was a partner in the New York firm of Barrett, Knapp, Smith, Schapiro, and Simon. In 1972 he was appointed United States District Court Judge.

In 1970, he was made Chairman of the New York City Commission to Investigate Alleged Police Corruption, and in 1972 this Commission published the well known Knapp Report, *Law and Order, A Study of the New York Police Department.*

Mr. Wilkins was born in St. Louis, Missouri, in 1901. Early in life he moved to St. Paul, Minnesota, where he attended public school. He graduated from the University of Minnesota in 1923. He was on the staff of the campus daily newspaper at the University of Minnesota and after graduation joined the staff of the *Call*, a weekly newspaper in Kansas City, Missouri.

In 1931 he joined the national staff of the National Association for the Advancement of Colored People as Assistant Secretary. While filling this position he became editor of *Crisis*, the official organ of the NAACP. In 1950 he was named Administrator of the NAACP and in 1955 he became its Executive Director.

He is the author of numerous articles for periodicals and his evaluations of various aspects of racial discrimination have appeared in such magazines as *McCalls,* the *New York Times Magazine* and the *Saturday Review.* He writes a weekly syndicated column which appears in daily newspapers across the country.

In 1967 he was awarded the Freedom Award by Freedom House and in 1969 he was one of 20 awarded the Medal of Freedom, the country's highest civil honor.

General Hubbard was born in San Francisco, California, in 1922. He attended public schools there. He holds a B.S. Degree in Military Science from the University of Omaha and an M.S. Degree in International Affairs from George Washington University.

He entered the Marine Corps in 1940 and was commissioned a Second Lieutenant two years later. He retired from the Marine Corps as a Brigadier General in November of 1972.

During World War II he served as an Infantry Officer in the South Pacific. He entered flight training in 1946 and the next year was designated as a Naval Aviator. He saw combat service in Korea during the Korean War as an Executive Officer of a marine fighter squadron. His assignments also included action in Vietnam and various staff positions at all levels. He holds the Silver Star, the Legion of Merit, the Distinguished Flying Cross and the Purple Heart.

He became Memphis Police Director on 1 December 1972.

In his article "Crime, Hypocrisy and the Just Society," Mr. Clark begins with a discussion of prohibition and its social failures. From that experience we concluded, he says, that we could not legislate morals and prevent acts which have no victims. But this is wrong thinking, he contends. All legislation involves moral judgment whether it be murder, theft, speeding, sale of impure food, bombing in Cambodia, racial discrimination, or exploitation of child labor. Moreover the acts of individuals which primarily affect themselves are not without their victims. To say that society has no interest in whether people hurt themselves is to make society a heartless place unable to solve its real problems or to offer fulfillment to its people. But we must face the fact that society cannot force people to live their private lives as it thinks best. Instead, society must create an environment in which freedom, equality, and justice prevail. When unenforceable statutes are removed from the books, the law can become an effective instrument for social change and a positive power for good.

Judge Knapp entitled his lecture, "Can the Universal Pervasiveness of Police Corruption be Obviated?" Very early he introduces Lincoln Steffins, "the turn of the century crusader and philosopher of corruption," and points up the similarity of his own findings on police corruption with those uncovered by Lincoln Steffins some seventy years before. But, whereas Steffins believed the problem of corruption to be an inevitable by-product of democracy and championed socialism as the ultimate solution, Judge Knapp believes the problem of corruption has not been solved because society simply has not been forced to solve it. At one time, Judge Knapp reasons, government was remote from people's day to day life. This is no longer true, and it may be that we have come to the stage where people can no longer tolerate corruption in government.

Judge Knapp is optimistic about change. He goes on

to outline how society must go about acting on the problem of corruption.

Mr. Wilkins chose as his topic, "The Search for Interracial Justice." He emphasized the concept of justice rather than crime. If we look at the dictionary meaning of justice we find permeating the concept is "the principle of just dealing." This gets Mr. Wilkins into the area of racial justice.

He traces the history of race relations in the United States since 1876 and the Hayes-Tilden compromise. He speaks of the founding of the NAACP in 1909 and of its record in the struggle for interracial justice. He discusses the problem as it relates to housing, public education, politics, job security and advancement. He concludes with a reference to President Lyndon B. Johnson and a quotation from one of his 1965 speeches.

General Hubbard spoke on "The Memphis Police Department." He began by citing some statistics that indicate the growth of the city and the demands placed on the local police department, and the extent to which the resources of the police department have grown. The lag is notable. He compares the resources of the police department to that of the city fire department. There again the comparison is unfavorable.

He goes on to cite four major criticisms of police departments today. Then he allows the patrolman to speak. This patrolman has four revealing statements to make about his work and how it affects the efficiency of the police department. Then General Hubbard speaks about some of the areas where innovative techniques are being applied—management, training, professionalism.

The Coordinating Committee of the series rendered service beyond the call of duty as this year's edition was planned and initiated. More particularly, they handled the task of selecting the general theme of the series and of selecting the speakers.

Special thanks go to several persons. First there is Mrs. Reva Cook who so very ably handled publicity for the series. Then there is Mr. Robert Garnett who acted as my assistant and as such especially ably managed the housing of the lectures. Thanks also go to Mrs. Gordon Lawhead who handled all the secretarial duties so expertly including the typing of this manuscript.

Mr. P. K. Seidman deserves a special vote of thanks. He financially underwrites the series as a memorial to his brother, the late M. L. Seidman. But in addition he actively participates in the day to day planning and conduct of the series.

Festus J. Viser
July, 1973

"Crime, Hypocrisy and the Just Society"

Lecture One*

by Ramsey Clark

Some day we will learn the world cannot be made safe for hypocrisy. We must face facts. Any other course of action in our interdependent society will prove perilous indeed.

There are few better illustrations of this proposition than our effort to use the penal sanction against what is today popularly called "victimless crime." The roll of conduct coming under the general concept includes a large part of all crime and the great majority of the activity of organized crime. The excessive use of alcohol, the use or possession for use of a wide range of drugs and narcotics, most types of gambling, prostitution, some types of sexual conduct, including homosexual acts,

*Mr. Clark was forced to cancel his lecture shortly before the lecture date. The following is a paper submitted by Mr. Clark for inclusion in this publication.

personal use or possession of pornographic materials, abortion and suicide are among crimes called victimless.

The major, most dramatic and disastrous effort by government in the United States to prohibit through the criminal sanction an individual's conduct of his own affairs was Prohibition: laws prohibiting the use of alcoholic beverages. The hypocrisy of the prohibition effort was enormous. We knew tens of millions of Americans used alcohol. We knew millions were alcoholic and we knew or soon learned they could not be prevented from drinking by the threat of jail, or fine. We were powerless to prevent widespread violations of the law which vastly diminished respect for its rule. Efforts to enforce the law necessarily resulted in discriminatory prosecutions which are inherently unjust and created fear and hatred of government. The rich could usually imbibe with impunity in their homes and at their clubs while the poor were prosecuted for trying to do as much. Because legitimate and cautious businessmen would not run the risks, the field was occupied by organized crime which increased its power and its wealth to its greatest empire in American history. Police and other officials in the system of criminal justice were widely exposed to corruption because the law was unenforceable and knowledge of its violation common. The health hazard from impure and dangerous alcoholic mixtures was increased greatly because of the risk and surreptitious nature of the business. When the absurdity of the effort at using the criminal sanction was finally faced, a constitutional amendment repealing prohibition passed three-quarters of the state legislatures within a single year. But the damage done to respect for law, the new power of organized crime and the corruption of law enforcement affect us still.

Observing the epoch of prohibition, many believed the error was our effort to legislate morals and to prevent acts which have no victims. The analysis is wrong. All legislation involves, consciously or otherwise, moral judgments. Legislative acts outlawing murder, theft, speeding, sale of impure food, bombing in Cambodia, racial discrimination and exploitation of child labor involve moral judgments.

Nor are the acts of individuals which affect themselves primarily without their victims. America has eight or nine million alcoholics. These persons are crippled by their sickness. Their family, friends and associates share their suffering: society itself bears much of the cost. It is not credible to say there are no victims of alcohol. Even if one's acts affect only himself, never entirely possible in society, he can be the victim of those acts.

Those who see no victims in suicides do not revere life. Suicide is not a private matter, alien to the interest of society. As few other indicia, it measures the quality of life in a society. Any person's death diminishes us.

It is not merely academic, or interesting, to observe that victimless crimes have victims and all law involves moral judgments. It is essential to understanding the nature and purpose of the social compact and the limits of the criminal sanction. If we say you cannot legislate morals, we deny the central purpose of law which is moral leadership. We then fail to make necessary and often difficult moral judgments consciously. If we contend there are not victims of drug addiction, gambling and prostitution, we repudiate what Earl Warren, the person who has done most in this time to enrich our lives with justice, has called the imperative need of the American people—"a political conception of compassion." To say society has no interest in whether people hurt themselves, that it is only when their conduct directly injures others that society is concerned, enshrines self-interest as the guiding principle of government. Such a country will be a heartless place, unable to solve problems or offer fulfillment to its people.

This does not mean we force individuals in their private conduct to do as we command. It only means we care for their well-being and will try through government to give them the chance for something better.

Such evasions denying the moral base of law and its concern for the individual involve an hypocrisy nearly as harmful as that which tells us we are effectively addressing a human problem when we make such acts as abortion a crime. It will not prevent pregnancy or make women want babies. Few acts of society are crueler, or inflict greater psychological violence, than seizing a sixteen-year-old girl, raised in the puritan ethic, and charging her with murder of a fetus.

No one favors abortion as an end in itself any more than open heart surgery on those with no need for it. Any just society will act to reduce the occasions on which abortions are needed, or wanted, to a minimum. This can be done by sex education, by prevention of rape and unwanted sexual relations and by the availability, understanding, and use of contraceptives. Where unwanted pregnancies occur we must face the issue of abortion squarely. History shows that to make abortion a crime will not prevent it. The rich may go to another country. The poor will seek ways here and be driven to means that jeopardize the life of the mother. Finally, to the unwanted child comes much of the same unhappiness in our society that led the mother not to want a child. There was no love, no family structure for support, no personal stability for raising children, little chance for a happy or a good life, and a high risk of child abuse and other experiences that lead to lives of misery and crime.

The need is to face the truth. The truth is you cannot force people to live their private lives as you say because you say so. First, society must strive to liberate its people from sickness, fear, and ignorance which causes them to act in ways harmful to themselves and others, to condemn as sin conduct they find more attractive than rectitude and simple decency, and to believe that in mass society millions can be prevented from doing what they wish by threat of force. Then society must move to create that environment in which freedom, equality and justice prevail. For there, the need of the people to escape from reality, to create a chance for happiness by dulling the senses through which they perceive life, to find a way to fulfillment by gambling for gold, will be reduced to a minimum. Reality will be bearable, happiness and fulfillment possible, in the nature of things.

There is no magic formula for knowing what is moral or immoral, good for people or bad for people, permissible and impermissible. In a free, democratic society, the people, through government, must make hard judgments, constantly scrutinize judgments made, and change judgments to conform to newly discovered truths. To condemn as criminal, or sick, homosexuality or the use of marijuana may satisfy an insentient people who hate what they call evil and favor economy in government, but it hardly answers questions about sexuality in modern society, or the effect of specific drugs on the human body. Old prejudices must yield to new truths without the agony of ostracizing individuals who may happen to be on the frontiers of changing mores. To wisely answer such issues we should approach them tolerantly with a positive philosophy, seeking liberty, quality in the lives of all, and justice. We should seek the truth without inhibition, aggressively, sceptically. The central question of our era is whether we can see the truth in time. We will demean human dignity if we deem sick those who choose to be homosexual or make criminal those who smoke marijuana until we can demonstrate by clear evidence the injury to the individual or society is unacceptable and that it can be effectively and constructively controlled by medical science or the criminal sanction. We have no such evidence.

The limited power of the criminal sanction, barely able to affect the problems of antisocial conduct where that conduct is directed at persons with a clear and direct conflicting interest, as in robbery or rape, simply cannot effectively apply to conduct where the interests of other members of society are not directly assaulted and where the activity is or can be private and personal. Where sympathies of affinity and consanguinity, mere personal embarrassment or the risk of harm from disclosure exceed the pain of concealment, people will not report unlawful conduct known to them. Effective law enforcement will always depend on a public support of the rule of law.

Today, most crime in America is never reported to police. The capacity of any system of criminal justice to prevent or control crime which is largely unreported is nil. The capacity of government to compel reporting of conduct which does no direct harm to adverse interests, which often involves substantial risk, and which cannot be prevented or controlled by the sanctions provided by law is nil. It further creates a climate in which the invasion of privacy is condoned by law which in turn makes enemies among the people and degrades law.

The ultimate criminal sanction is mainly force and segregation. Most will stand with Thoreau when he says "I was not born to be forced." Neither violence nor separation can solve such problems as alcoholism or addiction. These are complex social-medical problems. You cannot beat heroin from the bloodstream of an addict. You cannot dry a wino out by thirty days in the tank and expect him not to drink again. The absurdity of the law arresting a woman for prostitution for the fifty-fourth time and carrying her off to jail only reaffirms Dickens—if the law says that, the law is an ass. And when the law seeks to prohibit the desperately lonely or despondent individual from committing suicide by threatening jail, it shows again how punishment is a crime. It forgets how many people each year, incapable of suicide before imprisonment, find prison so inhumane they kill themselves. It fails to see the capacity of every individual to put himself beyond the jurisdiction of mortality and the incapacity of the State to police the waking moments of every citizen to prevent such escape.

We should eliminate scores of crimes from the statutes including those we generally call victimless crimes but not because the law can be meaningful without moral standard, or because we do not care if people hurt themselves. We should repeal statutes where the law is immoral, where it does not address a problem with which society should concern itself through law and if the penal sanction simply cannot help solve the problem involved.

To tell the people the problem can be solved by police and prisons is to mislead. As a result, we are diverted from the efforts essential to addressing the problem effectively, the system of criminal justice is diverted from problems it can help solve, the rule of law is exposed to ridicule and the system is corrupted. We diminish freedom, enforce inequality, and deny justice.

Nothing will more quickly destroy self-respect within a police service, or set police against society than law which imposes the duty to enforce the unenforceable, to harmfully interfere in people's private lives, to arrest and incarcerate again and again with no hope of curing alcoholism or addiction or preventing gambling or homosexual conduct. An officer proud to serve society will soon not be when he has to arrest the same drunk for the seventh time. Pick him up from the gutter by his broken wine bottle as if police were human garbage disposers. Tens of thousands of these arrests are made annually in most major cities. They consume a major part of all police time: their stock in trade.

The law can be an effective instrument for social change. In mass, urban, technologically advanced society, it must be. Other ways are not adequate alone to achieve the change in human attitudes and institutions which are essential to survival. Rights, fulfilled through the social compact, to health, education, employment, income and housing, can reduce alcoholism, addiction, prostitution and suicide. A political conception of compassion, written into the rule of law, renouncing greed and acquisitiveness and providing the essentials for decency in the human condition will reduce the desire to gamble.

The law can be a positive power for good, not a negative threat against evil. To be so, the law must provide moral leadership. It must state a generous and gentle purpose for the people. Then it will be respected. Then its promise can be fulfilled.

While law permits millions to dwell in poverty in the midst of affluence, the desire to gamble will be great. Great desires are not repressible by criminal sanctions. While the law seeks to prohibit conduct millions want to engage in, organized crime will provide the goods and services sought. Where organized crime flourishes, police and other agencies of criminal justice will be neutralized and corrupted in many exposed parts of the system. The corrosive effect can threaten the integrity of government, the stability of society and the chance to humanely address the underlying causes of the conduct that gives rise to greatest concern.

Thus, the need to decriminalize such conduct bears directly on our chance for freedom, for equality, and for justice. The way we address the issue will determine whether we are to be enslaved or free; whether we can affect our destiny; whether the law is to be an effective instrument for social change. For as Disraeli tells us, "We must choose to be the managers of change or the victims of change."

"Can the Universal Pervasiveness of
Police Corruption be Obviated?"

Lecture Two

by Whitman Knapp

When I was asked several months ago to give my remarks a title, I suggested a question, "Can the Universal Pervasiveness of Police Corruption be Obviated?" Of course, some time has passed since I made that suggestion, and not surprisingly the subject matter has become somewhat changed in emphasis in the course of preparing these remarks.

While police corruption will remain my focus, I shall try to relate it to the overall problem of corruption in the body politic, and also to put it into historical perspective. Both historical perspective and the relationship to the body politic were suggested by our own report.* On pages 4 and 5 of our preliminary summary we said:

"The problem of corruption is neither new, nor confined to the police. Reports of prior investiga-

*Law and Order, A Study of the New York Police Department (New York: George Braziller, Incorporated, 1972).

tions into police corruption, testimony taken by the Commission, and opinions of informed persons, both within and without the Department make it abundantly clear that police corruption has been a problem for many years. Investigations have occurred on the average of once in twenty years since before the turn of the century, and yet conditions exposed by one investigation seem substantially unchanged when the next one makes its report. This doesn't mean that the police have a monopoly on corruption. On the contrary, in every area where police corruption exists it is paralleled by corruption in other agencies of government, in industry and labor, and in the professions."

Of course we were referring only to New York City, which was the focus of our study, but I think the same statement would be applicable to practically any city in the nation.

So much for the relation of the problem to the ills of society in general. To put the matter in historical perspective, I should like to refer to Lincoln Steffens, the turn-of-the-century crusader and philosopher of corruption, who was sort of a one-man Knapp Commission. He investigated corruption, not only in New York, but in practically every major city in the land, and he published a series of articles, first about New York and then about various other cities. His great work began about two years before the turn of the century, and continued until the early days of Theodore Roosevelt's Administration. In 1931, he published an autobiography in which he tried to pull together the facts he had uncovered and to draw philosophic conclusions from them. The startling thing about his work is that the patterns of corruption he disclosed (and I am here confining myself to police corruption) in the City of New York were practically identical to the patterns we just now uncovered. There were the same systematic payments from gamblers, the same systematic payments from the liquor industry, as well as from prostitution. There were the same lists of contributors and the same methods of dividing up the take among the police officers involved. And this pattern, which he first discovered in New York, he found to exist in practically every city of the land. There was a difference in emphasis in those days. For example, the drug problem was not as pressing as it is now, prostitution seemed much more organized than today, building codes were not the problem they are now; but the patterns of corrupt payments were essentially the same.

When Steffens put all these things together in his autobiography, his philosophic conclusion was that corruption is an inevitable by-product of democracy in a capitalistic society. Democracy, Steffens concluded, is at once so hypocritical and so rigid that it cannot be made to work without corruption. His feelings about hypocrisy centered on the laws against gambling and prostitution. Significant numbers of the community did not want such laws enforced, and yet the electorate insisted on their being in existence. He also pointed to areas where regulation was conceded to be necessary but where the laws were too rigid to meet the demands, the legitimate and necessary demands, of a rapidly expanding economy. Railroads and utilities were the examples which Steffens gave of this phenomenon. When a railroad was to be built, it had to have a right-of-way and it had to have it quickly. Democracy, so he said, was so rigid that if one waited to proceed under the normal democratic process of going from legislature to legislature with explanation and persuasion, the railroad would never get built. And so corruption, not of policemen in that instance but of legislators, was, as he found, the inevitable answer.

Corresponding to the problems then faced by the railroads are those now confronting the building industry. In New York City today, a building cannot effectively be constructed without violating a host of regulations. The technique of pouring concrete, for example, now requires that a concrete truck park at the curb and pour concrete. Legislators have finally recognized that necessity, but the technique also requires that another truck be immediately behind, ready to move up and pour as soon as the first one stops. If there is any break in the flow of concrete, there are technical difficulties and the work must start all over again. The legislature, however, has never gotten around to dealing with that particular problem, so that the second truck and the third behind it are necessarily violating the law. The easiest way to deal with such a situation appears to be to slip a few bucks to the cop so that he will not give tickets.

Steffens' solution to such problems was socialism or communism. His solution was to eliminate the profit motive. He postulated that with the profit motive gone, the motive to corrupt would be gone, and corruption would disappear. I have no first hand experience with that approach, but I understand that it has not exactly worked out in some of the countries where it has been tried.

What, then, is the answer? Is Steffens correct in saying that the problem is insoluble in a capitalistic society? I suggest that such is not the case. The reason the problem has not been solved is that society has not yet been forced to solve it. As a general rule, society never deals with difficult problems until forced to do so. As an example, let us consider the problem of ecology. No one in Lincoln Steffens' day worried much about ecology. At that time people thoughtlessly polluted the atmosphere, polluted the rivers, dumped sewage into the ocean. They were not concerned because the air and the sea were thought to be inexhaustible. The rivers flowed into the ocean and nothing much mattered. Consequently, in those good old days when no one was concerned with pollution, trains ran up and down the valley, spewing out smoke and gas in a manner that no one would now conceive of tolerating. Today, the situation is different. Today, people realize that they must do something about ecology if they are to survive, and therefore they are forced to tackle the problem. Automobile manufacturers may not like it, and they may argue that the government is acting too fast or acting stupidly, but they do not suggest that nothing at all needs to be done. Fighting pollution is in their stockholders' interest as much as in anybody else's. Their stockholders not only want to get dividends; they also want to live. So automobile manufacturers, along with everyone else, are tackling the problem of pollution.

It is my suggestion that the problem of corruption may have advanced to the same stage as the problem of ecology, that is to say that the time may have come when society realizes that it is forced to confront it. In Lincoln

Steffens' day, corruption held a position more or less similar to ecology. Corruption was something that people got excited about every once in a while, and Lincoln Steffens made quite a reputation, and I guess a fortune, writing about it. But it did not vitally concern people. If the railroad bribed a few legislators to get a straight right-of-way, how did that really affect people in their daily lives? It did not. In those days government was a remote institution which did not really seem to affect the day-to-day life of the citizen. Therefore, the citizen could live with corruption. Perhaps the time has arrived when that is no longer possible. Government today impinges upon people's day-to-day existence, and it may just be that people can no longer tolerate its corruption.

As a minor example, consider the different impact of one aspect of police corruption in New York City today and at the turn of the century. The sections of the city then comparable to what are now sometimes referred to as "ghettos" were Irish enclaves. The police department was also predominantly Irish. Thus, corruption of the police department seemed to the ghetto resident more or less a method of siphoning money from the rich to the poor. Ghetto residents may have disapproved of their neighbor the cop who was collecting graft, but such disapproval was tempered by the admiring thought that the policeman was getting the money from "the other half," who should not have had it in the first place. That situation no longer exists. Policemen, in New York anyway, are no longer drawn from the ghetto but from predominantly middle-class, non-ghetto backgrounds. Nevertheless, the police still have the function of enforcing the law in the ghetto. So when they take graft they are no longer siphoning money into the ghetto but, on the contrary, may be seen as enriching themselves at the expense of the poor. This creates a hostility quite different from anything that was known in Steffens' time, and it creates problems that I do not have to dwell upon.

If I am correct in my hypothesis that society only acts when it is forced to (of course society does not make a conscious decision to start acting) and that such a necessity is now upon us in the area of corruption, one should be able to see significant differences between the situation in Steffens' day and the situation today. Indeed, one does. If one looks at the situation Steffens described, both as to the City of New York and as to all cities generally, the mayor and the police commissioner inevitably were shown to have been personal participants in the graft. The mayor and the police commissioner in all Steffens' reports, both in the City of New York and in every other city he examined, were shown to have personally participated in the division of corrupt money taken from gamblers and prostitutes and the liquor industry. Today, however, in the City of New York, with which I am familiar (and I presume the situation is generally the same elsewhere), there has not been any accusation of that kind since La Guardia had his cleanup campaign, which was before World War II. John Lindsay's bitterest enemy, and he has many, and Howard Leary's bitterest enemy, and he was the police commissioner who resigned shortly after our Commission was appointed, the bitterest enemy of either of these two men has never suggested—nor would there be the slightest evidence to support such a suggestion—

that either of them personally participated in the receipt of corrupt money. That fact indicates to me that there has been a change. The patterns may have been the same, the method of dealing with the dichotomy between that which society writes on its books and that which society enforces may have been the same, but no one during our investigation suggested that either the mayor or the police commissioner was personally involved in the receipt of corrupt money while everyone, quite correctly, simply took it for granted in Lincoln Steffens' day. And that difference seems to me somehow to validate my theory that society is beginning slowly to awaken to the need of doing something about corruption, and that there is movement in the right direction.

Maybe it is just wishful thinking that I see this change because I spent two years on this project, and they were not all easy years. I hate to think that it was all wasted, although that is a distinct possibility. However, I think the change does exist, and it encourages me to think of ways that society, when it feels the need, can meet the change.

If society is to act, it must realize that something has to be done and begin to think of ways to do it, exactly as people are now doing with respect to ecology. People must start focusing on the problem of what they actually want their laws to accomplish, and thus give realistic objectives to their police departments and other law enforcement agencies. And such focusing must take place in two areas, in what I call the moral area and what I call the industrial area. In the moral area, for example, people have to decide whether they want gambling or whether they do not. If people decide they want to stop gambling—and apparently no one really does want to—they have to see to it that everybody stops it. What people cannot realistically do is to say, "Okay, I can gamble, but you can't." As another example, prostitution has been around for quite a while. People have to start being realistic and decide what they are going to do about it. No American society has ever been willing to make a realistic appraisal of what to do about prostitution. Other societies have tackled the problem, I do not know with what success, certainly not complete success, but at least they have tackled it. No American society that I know of has ever tackled it. Then there is the problem of drugs, which is a *real* problem. In this area, it is obviously wrong to say that just because laws tend to produce corruption they should necessarily be repealed. The easiest way to eliminate corruption, at least police corruption, would be to repeal the penal law, but obviously no one wants to do that. In the drug situation, people have to devote hard thinking to exactly what their objectives are. If society equates marijuana with heroin and has the same general laws applicable to both, as many states do and the federal government in essence does, society not only invites corruption but also invites complete breakdown of enforcement procedures. I am no expert on the correct solution of the drug problem. I do know, however, that there is a difference between heroin and marijuana. That I can tell you without being an expert. I do not know whether society should legalize marijuana, although a growing body of opinion seems to think that it is less harmful than alcohol. I certainly do not know what the final solution about heroin is; many persons will argue that it should be dealt with as the English do, in a permissive manner, but never having had direct experience with the English method I can not express an opinion on it. I do know this, however: if people narrow the field of enforcement so as to have a small, manageable heroin enforcement apparatus rather than a broad-scale, hit-or-miss apparatus that covers marijuana and every other drug, then society would have some chance of limiting its area of supervision and keeping corruption in some sort of check.

In the industrial area the answer is much easier, and I have already suggested it. Society cannot just draft general legislation and leave it to the police to work it out as best they can, making exceptions wherever they think it expedient. Society must enact workable laws and provide legal ways of relief from those laws when necessary. For example, a statute cannot be written which envisages all the problems that will over the years be encountered in constructing a building. Legislators cannot draft a law today which is going to fit exactly the technology that will exist five years from now—how to park vehicles, how to rig, how to do this or that. But legislators can build into the law legitimate ways of getting relief from rigidities as they develop. As of now, no one has bothered to do that. They just leave the law rigid, and corruption begins to creep in.

In the meantime, what about the police administrator who has to deal with today's police department? He cannot wait for the legislature to get around to do those things which, if I am correct in my assumptions, ultimately must be done. The police administrator has the immediate responsibility for a department.

But why emphasize the police? Why not talk about the building department, which, in New York at least, is probably more corrupt. Why not talk about the health department, or various other departments where there is the same problem. Why do we always talk about the police? The reason is that the police force is the most sensitive organ of government. The average citizen knows exactly what the neighborhood cop does, and knows his personal impact. As far as the majority is concerned, the cop *is the law*. In contrast, what I do in the United States District Court in the Southern District of New York does not matter to most people; they have never heard of me in my capacity as a judge and they never hope to. But the cop on the beat represents government at work.

A complicating problem facing the police administrator is the extremely complex nature of a metropolitan police force, which is ingrown, and for very obvious reasons. Policemen think they live in a sea of hostility, and in fact they do. This hostility applies not only to those assigned to high crime areas, but to police generally. If someone should wake you up in the middle of the night, and say, "Cop," you would not immediately get a picture of a benevolent fellow in blue who is protecting your home against burglary. Rather, you would picture someone who is giving you a ticket. Nobody, whether he is a Sunday motorist or a burglar, likes to have his activities interfered with, and therefore his instant reaction to cops is one of hostility. Now that is a phenomenon that policemen live with from day to day, and as human beings they react against it by being ingrown. This phenomenon produces an intense loyalty within the department. If understood properly, such loyalty could be appealed to as a factor in the fight against corruption; but if misunderstood or ignored, it results in what we found in New York when we started our investigation, a blank wall against any suggestion from the outside.

The first thing to accomplish, and this much I think we did accomplish, is to give the police a real confidence that the citizen has a bona fide expectation that they will respond to a call for honesty. The administrator can accomplish this by being direct and perhaps ruthless, but at all times fair. Eventually, policemen will begin to get the idea that the "establishment" is paying them the compliment of taking seriously their own desire to be honest, and they will respond by taking affirmative action of their own.

As I said in my introduction, a sizeable majority was involved in the corruption our Commission uncovered, and I do not mean in just taking free cups of coffee, I mean in real corruption. But I do not mean to suggest that a sizeable majority gets any great income out of corruption. It does not. The corrupt policemen who hit the headlines when caught with fifty or a hundred thousand dollar extortions from heroin dealers represent an infinitesimal fraction of corrupt policemen. The only way to deal with that kind is to catch and jail them. However, the vast majority fall into corruption just because it is easier to do it than not to, and their income from corruption is not sizeable in the sense that it would ruin their standard of living if taken away from them. It would cut it down, but it would not ruin it. We became convinced from our experience that a vast majority of those who were engaged in serious corruption (any corruption beyond a free cup of coffee or a free meal is serious) would prefer to exchange what they get by corruption for the return luxury of self-respect. The police administrator must meet the challenge of invoking that desire for self-respect. Our suggestion to the City of New York, and whether it applies to smaller locales I am not sure, is that the police department follow the lead of the Internal Revenue Service and organize within itself an independent inspection unit. In the unit within the IRS there are special agents who have no concern at all whether or not any individual pays taxes, but whose sole concern is whether any person shall encourage a revenue agent to be corrupt. The special agents are concerned only with potential corruption, and they have no concern with the raising of revenue. Therefore, they are not in a camaraderie with those that must raise revenue. However, they are responsible to the same commissioners, so there is no division of authority. This special unit was established in the Revenue Service at the close of the Truman administration pursuant to the recommendation of the King Committee, a senatorial committee which made an investigation of the Revenue Service similar to ours of the police department. Since then, the IRS, as far as I am aware, has been reasonably free of corruption. And why? Not because taxpayers are any more inherently law-abiding than barkeepers, but because every taxpayer and every accountant, or lawyer, or anybody else that deals with the Revenue Service knows that the fellow he is talking to may not be an agent out to get his taxes, but may be an agent out to find evidence of potential corruption. Such knowledge has a very salutary effect on the taxpayer and on the agent, who is aware that his buddy may be a member of the special unit.

Another recommendation we made was that there be as much emphasis on catching the fellow who agrees to a shakedown, or agrees to a bribe, as on the fellow who receives it; and that there be as much emphasis on any lawyer, businessman or judge who gets involved in corruption as on the policeman who becomes corrupt. The police have a perfectly legitimate complaint that they are the ones who are always under the spotlight. We therefore recommended, on a temporary basis at least, that a special unit of the attorney general's office be established with the sole purpose of going after corruption not only in the police department but in every other agency or person touching upon the criminal justice system—judges, lawyers, police, laymen.

This drive has been effective in New York, and on a short range, at least, the police department has responded to it. Now the question is, have we had any permanent effect? My answer is: "You ask me that fifteen years from tonight."

"The Search for Interracial Justice"

Lecture Three

by Roy Wilkins

A natural question is, what is justice? What is interracial justice? Is the latter a general term or is it one that applies with special significance to the restlessness between the races in the United States?

The preferred definition in the Oxford Universal Dictionary says, "The quality of being (morally) just or righteous; the principle of just dealing; just conduct; integrity, rectitude." The second definition which merges with the preferred one, in the minds of most of us is, "Exercise of authority or power in maintenance of right; vindication of right by assignment of reward or punishment. The administration of law, or the forms and processes attending it . . . infliction of punishment, legal vengeance on our offender . . ." The phrase, "to do justice to (a person or thing); to render one what is his due, or vindicate his just claims . . ."

So, interracial justice, which we will review tonight, is mostly justice, our standard definition of it, with perhaps some special conditions and overtones which we will touch upon later. It is the contention of these remarks that the continued violation of the human rights of Negro Americans threatens the basic principles upon which this nation was founded. If the nation should fail in its quest for interracial justice, we would have not even the great declarations on human freedom to be found in our cherished documents. We would be something less, something different from the United States of America as we have known it down through the two centuries of our existence.

Our world would be a different and worse place if we should lose this particular battle. Needless to say, the peoples of the world who look to the leadership of the United States, citing our famed declarations of human freedom, to bring more justice into the world's dealings will have their hopes dashed.

We had given up on interracial justice in 1876, the time of the Hayes-Tilden compromise. Our central government in Washington agreed to forget all the blood and travail of the war of 1861-65. The national leadership then threw in the towel in the effort to apply the Constitution and its high-sounding language to the newly-freed slaves. Instead, we embarked on a course of strict separation of the races. We did not care that it was not just. Our industrial states wanted to be about nation-building. Our cotton states wanted to rebuild their shattered economy.

So, in 1896, the U. S. Supreme Court, held, in *Plessy v. Ferguson*, that the U. S. Constitution could be satisfied with white-black separatism. In all things social, said Dr. Booker T. Washington in an Atlanta Exposition speech in 1895, the races can be as separate as the fingers, "yet one as the hand in all things essential to mutual progress." Even those who look back upon Washington and attempt to understand his difficult position, must admit that there was little interracial justice in his proposal. It did offer to have the Negro give up political activity, including the precious right to the franchise, and, too, all efforts to secure an adequate education, including college. In return he was to become a laborer, a worker in the skilled as well as the unskilled categories.

In his lone dissenting opinion in the Plessy case, Mr. Justice Harlan said that enactment of laws by other states similar to that under review in Louisiana "would be in the highest degree mischievous." He declared further that laws would place "in a condition of legal inferiority a large body of American citizens . . ."

"Legal inferiority" means, among other things, that the ordinary concepts of justice are not applied to any dealings involving black and white citizens.

It was in this atmosphere that the Niagara Movement of a few Negro intellectuals met in 1905. It was in the alarm created by the Springfield, Illinois, riot of 1908 that the National Association for the Advancement of Colored People, an interracial association, was organized in 1909. Shortly after its founding, it was joined by the Niagara Movement.

The NAACP was essentially a movement for interracial justice, for the motivating principle was to deal justly, to deal with integrity and rectitude; to vindicate the just claims of a submerged people; to exercise authority or power in maintenance of right. The forms and processes attending the administration of law were to be invoked. A long, slow climb from 1896 conditions to 1973 conditions was undertaken.

It has been said that the NAACP is a body dedicated to action in the Courts. This, of course, does not mean that other methods of protest were not employed. The record of the NAACP abounds with picketing, marching, demonstrations, protest rallies, lobbying and selective buying campaigns. The Association staged what was probably the first marching protest in 1917. Some 15,000 persons, predominately black, marched in a silent protest parade down New York's Fifth Avenue carrying signs against the crime of lynching.

But the situation of the Negro citizens was so precarious with respect to justice, to life itself, that major emphasis was placed on reiterating their legal position as citizens, on the general administration of justice, extradition (in the early days), police methods and sentencing. Very early, too, attention was given the racial composition of the prison population. Almost at once was to come an interest in legislation and political activity aimed at badly-needed legislation, but also at the executives (individuals and parties) that used legislation in ways deemed to be unjust to the black minority.

Something less than interracial justice was involved in the cases of nineteen or twenty young Negro sailors on the aircraft carrier, *Kitty Hawk*. This case is a perfect illustration of the fact that, even though an improvement has occurred in naked injustices on account of race, the search for interracial justice is still far from that goal. Much activity of the NAACP must continue to be in search of justice.

In October 1972 two days of fighting took place between the white and black personnel of the carrier. Only one white sailor was arrested and charged, and he was quickly acquitted. For three weeks the arrested young black sailors were allowed to go about their normal tasks. Suddenly, the nineteen who had asked for NAACP legal help were bundled into a plane and flown to San Diego. There they were confined to the brig in pre-trial confinement.

Despite strenuous protest, in and out of court, this confinement was continued. The men could not have received, even if found guilty, sentences more severe than the brig-time they were serving in pre-trial confinement.

But the event which infuriated young black civilians and armed services personnel was the revelation that the conviction of at least one black sailor had been obtained through the perjured testimony of a white sailor. The Navy acted promptly and reversed the conviction. It also changed the black sailor's discharge to honorable. Of course, the Navy said the reversal was due to a "routine review" and not to the revelation of perjury. But more than a nagging suspicion exists among black citizens that there was "dirty pool" in this particular case and in other *Kitty Hawk* cases. Why, if there was a fight between white and black sailors were only blacks arrested?

A Task Force on racial tensions in the armed services has found that discriminations are rife. Many black servicemen are, like most soldiers, sailors and airmen, given to griping. However, there is more than enough evidence to suggest that in their complaints of racial unfairness, most black servicemen are correct. The stockade population, heavily black, pre-trial confinement, promotions, housing, differences in punishment for the same crime and the free use of discharges other than honorable all form a basis for the racial differences black servicemen cite. The Department of Defense has recognized that some complaints are legitimate and has several remedial programs underway.

The *Kitty Hawk* cases in 1972-1973 mirror many of the same complaints (with only the crassness absent) that the Arkansas Sharecroppers' Case brought to the fore in 1919-23, just fifty-odd years ago. Has there been progress in the search of interracial justice? Is there any basis for the sweeping assertions by radical blacks that the race is just where it was decades ago, that nothing essential has changed, that today we are simply less harsh and less peremptory, but that the results are the same. This researcher does not happen to believe that this is true, but the parallels are there.

In October 1919 black sharecroppers were conferring with a Negro attorney, trying to get a better price for their cotton. Several cars went by the church and a gun was fired into the meeting. A sharecropper fired back and a white man was killed.

Quickly the exchange was labeled an "insurrection." Troops were called out and whites were deputized to shoot Negroes indiscriminantly. Twelve men were sentenced to death by a kangaroo court and sixty-seven to long terms in prison. Defense attorneys were allowed not more than two minutes with each defendant. The jury was out less than five minutes, and the sentences were the same as those in the kangaroo court.

Four years later all the men were freed when the U. S. Supreme Court held that the black men had not been accorded due process of law because the "spirit of the mob" was heavy in the courtroom. Was this decision, applicable to every defendant, black or white, a beginning of the bringing of interracial justice out of the brusque, unthinking racial discriminations that soiled —and still soils—our system of justice?

In housing the encounters have been long and sharp and the progress has been slow. One of the first cases to be taken to the Supreme Court by the young NAACP arose in Louisville, Kentucky, in 1917. A municipal ordinance, in which a city council set up racially segregated areas, prevented the sale of a house owned by a white man to a black purchaser. The white owner sued, claiming that the ordinance was depriving him of the use of his property solely because of race. He won and segregation, at least by municipal ordinance, was declared to be unconstitutional.

During the Twenties and Thirties housing disputes were sharp, and in 1925 Dr. Ossian H. Sweet, a Negro doctor in Detroit, on moving into his new house was surrounded by a howling mob. A shot was fired from inside the house and one member of the mob was killed. Clarence Darrow was brought in as defense counsel by the NAACP and Henry Sweet was acquitted in 1926.

But the really tough item in the crusade for freedom and justice in housing was the covenant between white owners of houses. They agreed among themselves not to sell to a Negro or some other non-white. These covenants were enforceable in the courts. Other signers could bring suit against any signer who weakened. What the Supreme Court did in *Shelley v. Keaemer*, in 1948, was to rule that whereas the owners were free to covenant together, the courts could not enforce such agreements because such action was contrary to the guarantees of the Constitution. Thus, owners could still draw up agreements, but if one of them decided to break his promise, no one could sue and make it stick.

A part of the answer to the plight of 22 million Negro Americans is a decent home in decent surroundings. If they do not have access to a home, they are the victims of racial injustice. A task of anyone who seeks justice for a race is to remove the artificial barriers that either exclude members of that race from home ownership or charge them an extra amount for access to shelter.

What is justice in the matter of employment? How does race enter into the securing and holding of the kind of employment that will make a victim of discrimination able to provide for his family's needs? What will convince him that the broad effort for justice includes his earning the money to pay for the home at his level of income?

One of the widely-favored methods of management is to insist, for prospective black employes, on a test. Tests are given for everything—promotions, new jobs, new seniority. Just as the Negro worker was getting his fill of frustration, the courts have held that tests must be job-related. Time was (and it is still a practice) when Negroes who wanted a promotion were asked about Beethoven, Mozart and Shakespeare. Now the U. S. Supreme Court has held in *Griggs v. Duke Power Company* that the tests must have a relation to the job.

In *Banks v. Lockheed*, a court has changed the upward mobility at the plant and awarded a sum of money to compensate (on a small scale) for the slowness of promotion with its attendant racial bias. As for separate racial seniority, the Bethlehem Steel Company plant at Sparrows Point, Maryland, has been instructed to change its system for one that is more just.

Public education is laced through with difficult decisions on justice and injustice in racial matters. There is no difficulty on the broad question. It is where one gets into politics, into personal ambition and greed for power, and into the home-mother-family-religion complex that hard questions enter.

It is easy to determine that black Americans have been discriminated against in public education for decades. We have only to cite per capita expenditures. Before the decision of 17 May 1954 there was a saying among Negroes that only the Washington, D. C., and St. Louis segregated school systems could be mentioned in any discussion of segregation. It was recognized that even these two were not nearly equal.

Today is just one month short of nineteen years since segregated schools were declared to be unconstitutional. We have shilly-shallied back and forth and considerable desegregation has taken place, but the notion is far short of the goal. Here in Memphis a plan has been presented by three school board members and the NAACP by which every school in the system will be desegregated. In contrast, the school board plan will leave nineteen all-black elementary schools, four junior high and two high schools.

Outside of Memphis, in northern and western cities, school administrators are dragging their feet on desegregation and the South, reluctant as it has been, may yet beat non-Dixie systems. The key word now is the transportation of school pupils. Although the Supreme Court unanimously approved busing as a constitutional tool for dismantling the dual system in the Charlotte case, everyone is waiting the Court's opinion in the Detroit, Michigan, and Richmond, Virginia, appeals. The cities are squirming and the legislative bodies are hemming and hawing, but there is only one choice if the 1954 decision to give the black child equality is to be made real. Either there must be "instant" equality in the neighborhood schools or there must be busing.

As might have been expected, a field in which there appears to be a good chance of achieving justice on many interracial fronts is that of the ballot. In fact, there is a definite trend toward use of the franchise as a weapon, rather than disengagement or violence. There are now about 2,000 elected black officials in the nation. Others occupy appointive offices. Once a black mayor was a rarity; now there are many.

There are fifteen black Congressmen, including three women—one from New York, one from Texas and one from California. There is one Negro U. S. Senator from Massachusetts, a state with only three percent black population. Every Southern state has black faces in its legislature. The Black Panthers have dropped the violence and the guns, and Bobby Seale, their national head, is running today (17 April) for mayor of Oakland, California. Black voters are concentrating on local candidates and on local issues. They are building, consciously, political power.

The shift will not affect matters overnight, but if

political control is achieved in more and more areas, the trend-setters will win out over the windbags and the blusterers. Certain it is that not since the eruptions of the Sixties have prospects been so bright for the fruitful ballot being substituted for unproductive (except backlash) threats to peace and progress.

This has been only a partial story of the search for interracial justice. The whole tale is immense, as large as the grand concept of our nation's destiny. Only a few areas have been sketched, a few details inked in. It must be apparent to everyone that there is a special quirk to interracial justice in America. Our white people, whether they come from Minnesota or Mississippi, have certain deeply-ingrained attitudes about race which they have learned at their mother's knee. The schools and the textbooks have not helped them much with their habitual biases. Our minorities, especially our black minority, have their attitudes and their prejudices.

It remains the conviction of this observer that advances have been made. Often these are not visible, being buried in the mood of the day. They are there, however, and they speak up at the most unusual times.

We had, a few years ago, a President who hailed from Texas and talked in the drawl of his region. But for the first time from the White House, he espoused the cause of interracial justice. In June 1965 Lyndon Baines Johnson spoke frankly and feelingly on the subject that concerns us tonight. He declared:

> For what is justice?
> It is to fulfill the fair expectations of man.
> Thus, American justice is a very special thing.
> For, from the first, this has been a land of towering

expectations. It was to be a nation where each man could be ruled by the common consent of all—enshrined in law, given life by institutions, guided by men themselves subject to its rule. And all—all of every station and origin—would be touched equally in obligation and in liberty.

And beyond this was the dignity of man. Each could become whatever his qualities of mind and spirit would permit—to strive, to seek and, if he could, to find his happiness.

This is American justice. We have pursued it faithfully to the edge of our imperfections. And we have failed to find it for the American Negro.

It is the glorious opportunity of this generation to end the one huge wrong of the American Nation and, in so doing, to find America for ourselves, with the same immense thrill of discovery which gripped those who first began to realize that here, at last, was a home for freedom."

"The Memphis Police Department"

Lecture Four

by Jay Hubbard

It is a flattering but somewhat intimidating experience to follow such distinguished authorities as Justice Tom Clark, Judge Whitman Knapp and Mr. Roy Wilkins. I would be more comfortable in less competent company where my own lack of credentials would not be quite so apparent. But I do have one thing in common with the first three speakers in this lecture series and that is great appreciation to the Seidman Family for sponsoring the presentations. Moreover, the timeliness of their topic this year is almost uncanny.

Having enjoyed the first three lectures myself, I only wish I could be sitting out there with you for this final session since I know of no one in this city who is more in need of listening rather than talking.

Now, having exhibited due modesty, I will tear into the question of the police role in crime and justice and tell you exactly how it all should be done. I shall do it by remaining more operational than philosophical and by admitting that my own concepts on today's police function are heavily influenced by Charles B. Saunders, Jr., formerly of the Brookings Institution, who wrote *Upgrading the American Police* and by Dr. J. F. Elliott, of the General Electric Company, Syracuse, New York, who authored *The "New" Police*. I also have drawn on the *Knapp Commission Report*, a November 1972 *Progress Report* from the Police Foundation on experiments in police improvement and the *Law Enforcement Booklet for Police* which is co-authored by Lewis B. Schwartz, Law Professor, and Stephen R. Goldstein, Associate Law Professor, both of the University of Pennsylvania.

But the most compelling influence on the views I will present stem from observations through my own lifetime, sharpened by the focus of these past five months where I have actually assumed some responsibility for a police operation. I am also a believer in the oft quoted assertion that "nothing is stronger than an idea whose time has come." I suggest that the previous speakers in this year's Seidman Series also subscribe to that view, each in his own way. For example, Justice Clark told us that real change comes only after all of the more comfortable alternatives have failed. Judge Knapp left no doubt in our minds about the urgency of reform in metropolitan police departments and Mr. Wilkins, in his characteristically quiet but powerful way, stressed the point that minorities will no longer tolerate inequities, either within a police department in terms of insuring equal opportunity for minority officers, or in the way police exercise authority toward minorities.

Memphis' starring role in national crime statistics is a nagging reminder to everyone in this city that the problem has finally reached proportions here in the city of good abode that can no longer be tolerated. To quote from a Broadway musical of some years ago, "There's trouble right here in River City"—so much trouble that citizen action groups are beginning to pick up a long neglected share of the burden that each business, each neighborhood and each local institution bears in deterring crime in any city, large or small.

Let me just cite a handful of statistics to give you a feel for the order of increase in demands on the Memphis Police Department over the past five years:

> From 1968 through 1972, Memphis' population increased about 20% and in geographic area, about 33%. Commissioned police officer strength increased less than 1% during the same period.
>
> The number of calls for police assistance increased in approximately direct proportion to population growth, about 20%. In numbers, that is 410,000 calls during calendar year 1972. However, many incidents that formerly would require the dispatching of officers were being handled by telephone, so the actual number is even higher.
>
> Serious crime increased 63% during the period.
>
> Traffic accidents increased 35% from 25,052 in 1968 to 33,912 in 1972, and killed or injured

increased at approximately the same rate, from 6,578 to 9,396.

In 1968 our Criminal Investigation Division was staffed by 78 officers who handled 12,029 cases. Last year those Bureaus had 77 officers trying to deal with a 66% increase, or 1806 additional cases. You can be sure that clearance rates suffered.

We are all proud of the Memphis Fire Department, for good reason—it is one of the best in the country. Their budget, every year since 1961, has exceeded the police budget on an average of 10% each year. In most cities, the reverse is consistently true. This is not presented as a complaint, but only to suggest part of the answer to the growing success of crime. I may as well blurt it out and say that when the community is as concerned about crime as it is about fire, then we will be on the road to recovery.

I will not belabor the need for better civic support any further because I believe the awakening has come. Whether we will doze off again remains to be seen. We do know that when all of the civilian and police elements in a community join together to prevent crime, the product is synergistic—where the total effective force created is significantly larger than the sum of the individual efforts exerted by each component. We can use some of that synergistic phenomenon right here and now—in the *positive* direction.

Contemporary Criticisms of and by Police

The problem, of course, is not limited to Memphis. Our ascendancy to the top of the list of crime-ridden large cities resulted from getting "behinder and behinder" as the years ticked by. Police departments are especially sensitive to changing political tides and critically dependent upon the annual budget that the politicians devise. The history of underfunding police is as common as underfunding education used to be. Again, that was more a national than a local problem. I am not familiar with the history of how long it took Memphis to turn the corner in support for education, but it is crystal clear that the time for drastic action in law enforcement funding has arrived. We will eventually reverse the crime statistics, but it will take more than one or even two immensely generous budget years because more than money is involved and because we have allowed ourselves to fall five to ten years behind most other cities of similar dimensions and none of those are enjoying anything close to a free environment yet. I believe that Memphis is almost uniquely endowed to defeat crime through unified effort and a truly respected police department. That is the good news. We are still of manageable size and blessed with a southern heritage of local pride and respect for law.

Before diving directly into current Memphis Police Department issues and goals, I will try to synthesize current major criticisms of police departments today. These typify what consistently recur in the literature and in public discussion:

> Police lack both appreciation and competence for sound management.
>
> Their organizational structure, resource allocation and tactical operations are stereotyped and unimaginative.

> They are not adequately trained to deal in today's complex environment and, therefore, are neither compensated nor respected as true professionals should be.
>
> They are internally defensive, gossip prone and highly resistant to change.

These characteristics, if true, can in various combinations help explain why this incredibly important element of our society is generally undermanned, underequipped and hardly understood by many of the communities that they are dedicated to serve. I will leave it to each of you to decide how much or how little these criticisms fit Memphis, but as part of that department I would strenuously object to any notion that it all applies across the board. Such generalization is unwarranted, and we have already absorbed enough such broadsides recently. I believe that most any Memphis Police Officer would agree that we do have pockets of resistance to change, that we do have some amount of ongoing corruption, and that we do abuse authority, both racially and youth directed. But he will not agree that the department is basically corrupt or sadistic.

Today, the woods are full of fresh new experts challenged by the complexity of the law enforcement problem. We have two and four year offerings in colleges and universities and graduate programs are not far off. We are applying operations analysis techniques to insure more effective application of resources. But before fully submitting to this much needed fresh wave of attention from the outside, let's hear from a patrolman. He will tell you that:

- The public and their chosen officials have never, ever given him anything close to what his task calls for in manpower, equipment and competitive career incentives.
- Neither does he have fully rational laws that he can enforce with total conviction knowing that the courts will back him to the hilt.
- The outsider can never really understand the internal peer pressures that can gradually turn an idealistic young patrolman into a cynical compromiser in the space of a few years—in some cases, a few months.
- Neither can an outsider appreciate how much abuse is directed at police officers today. The public never seems to hear about the countless times an officer keeps his cool or risks his neck, but let him take one swipe with his baton and it's all over town, with the worst possible interpretation.

Management

This has probably been the weakest single area in our department, but it is also the one which can be corrected most rapidly. Planning, programming and budgeting are simply not that difficult, once a basic structure is defined and formats prescribed. Violations of sound management principles are evident at every level of responsibility and are too numerous to detail here. Let me give you a few insights. First of all, the Chief of Police had a span of control that dealt with two principal subordinates while each of those harried executives had as many as twelve separate functions reporting to him. Among the responsibilities under the former Deputy Chief for Administrative Services was looking out for a 1.5 million dollar fleet of vehicles. He had a man who ran the police lot but no primary vehicle manager to plan and budget for orderly maintenance and replacement of vehicles, which constitute the single most important material resource we have. As a matter of fact, there was not even anything as basic as a preventive maintenance program. As a result the vehicles ran until they literally screamed for repair. I can tell you that those deficiencies are being cured post haste. I should also mention that we now plan to replace patrol units at 50,000 miles and transportation units every other year. We have kept our patrolmen in full-size squad cars in the belief that this is a vital part of their weapons system and no place to impose arbitrary economics. On the other hand, we are standardizing the transportation vehicles in medium economy models.

As for basic organization, we have kept the many good parts of the old structure and revised the rest. We have delegated more authority and have expanded from two to three Deputy Chiefs with narrower, more clearly defined areas of responsibility. The Bureaus under these Deputies have been strengthened and refocused. We have decentralized more authority and responsibility to our Precinct Commanders so that they will now be fully accountable within their geographic areas for traffic enforcement, uniform patrol, initial investigations and community relations. We have added an inspection function, which reports only to the Chief and to the Director, to poke around the Department to render assistance and to check on integrity and efficiency. At our recent budget hearing before the Budget Committee of the City Council, every Bureau Commander was present and well prepared to defend his own budget elements. I believe that just the knowledge of that preparation gave Council members increased confidence in our expression of requirements for fiscal 1974.

We believe that cleaned up functional lines and stronger delegation of authority are already producing a management team capable of leading this department out of its past hand-to-mouth, reaction oriented approach to competing with other city agencies for the limited funding available. We feel that this constitutes the best form of frontal attack against crime producing activity by having us better organized and equipped to deal with it. Our new organization devotes over 90% of its commissioned manpower to operational effort, thereby placing emphasis in the right place. The number of commissioned officers devoting their full time to supporting administrative, logistical and planning duties is about 9%. That includes a new Planning, Research and Analysis Bureau which I call the "skunk works." That group is to be targeted against inefficiency and inequity whether it be in management, resource allocation or tactics. We will come to expect great things from this group once it establishes momentum. It will be augmented by officers of various ranks from the Precincts and Operational Bureaus to insure current tactical realism in the ideas that we want them to generate.

Tactical Operations

If our management efforts constitute the broad frontal effort to defeat crime, then our tactical operations are the flanking attack that is needed against specific objectives. While the greatest strength in the Memphis Police Department lies in its tactical ability—which has been proven many times—and this includes investigation as well as uniform patrol, we have at the same time fallen into the trap of becoming stereotyped. There are some procedures and approaches that are basic and, therefore, difficult to improve upon, but there is also an emerging body of technology and techniques that tell us we had better get with the 1970s in some of our operational concepts. For example, we still assign resources more on the basis of rotational shift tours of duty and balanced distribution to the precincts than we do based on time, space and criminal activity levels. All I can do is assure you that we are conscious of this natural tendency to follow set patterns and that we are looking for fresh approaches. We will be better able to experiment as more manpower and vehicles become available in the months ahead. One obvious deterrent to innovation is that we seem to be caught in the tight web of a defensive posture. When resources are scarce and the demand for their services remains high, you become stymied against taking bold new initiatives. Nevertheless, we believe we can do better— even with what we have already—and we intend to. As we bring new communications, information, transportation and management systems on the line, we will begin to run out of excuses.

Training

Some very exciting pressures are gaining momentum all over the country in trying to advance both basic training standards and follow-up workshops, seminars and instruction. But I can tell you that there is no single police academy or private law enforcement or criminal justice training curriculum in this country that is fully satisfied with itself. In seeking the answers that are so urgently needed, the important thing is that the search has never been more intense. I believe we can expect results in the same way that American productivity and ingenuity has always somehow managed, usually under pressure, to come up with the solutions that the times and the people demand.

We are probing the entire question of how best to stimulate and prepare young men and women for careers in law enforcement and how to enrich both their initial training and follow-up studies. The Academy class now in session is in its next to last week in a twelve week curriculum. We expanded from an eight week course by injecting large doses of behavioral science. We are well aware that this curriculum is being criticized by the class to such extent that we should not simply repeat it for the next group. Each new class should expect to have its own unique curriculum—hopefully improving on what went before.

Our longer term training goals here in Memphis extend well beyond that. We hope, within the next few years, to raise one of the most modern Police Training Academies in the nation right here in Memphis. We also hope to parallel it with a crime laboratory of equal quality. These goals flow from the belief that Memphis, as the economic center of gravity for the entire mid-south, has a clear responsibility to take the initiative in putting together whatever is required to improve the effectiveness of law enforcement throughout that large and important region. Memphis State and Shelby State both reinforce the feasibility of doing it here. We do not regard this as a threat to the state operated police training academy at Donelson, Tennessee. That institution cannot now fully serve present needs within the state. Meanwhile, the tri-state region is becoming more closely bound together in terms of law enforcement because crime flows through and within the area without regard for state boundaries or politics. We hope to apply our new computerized criminal justice information system, which will begin operation this fall, eventually to serve less endowed cities and towns throughout the region by allowing them to rent computer terminals that will satellite on the Memphis-Shelby County System. There is no question but that the Memphis Police Department is looked to by many of these communities as having a distinct leadership responsibility. We have continual contact and cooperation with one another throughout each year. We share intelligence information and even help train some of their officers now, but our training facility is limited and outmoded. A number of Chiefs of Police of smaller communities are alumni of the Memphis Police Department—a natural source for such leadership. We will need a great deal of support to bring the new academy and crime lab into being, but we believe that the logic and need for such regional services will eventually make it happen. That's a long way from what we have today—a facility that basically belongs to the Fire Department and a record of zero capital outlay for the Memphis Police Academy in five years.

Professionalism

We could become lost in a maze of definitions right at the start, so I must ask that you accept a fairly narrow concept of what we mean by professionalism. Would you agree that the minimum elements that characterize a profession are that it requires some specific academic qualifications for entry and that it carries an obligation to adhere to both performance and ethical standards? Would you also grant that a profession is expected to contain within itself both the mechanism and the willingness to enforce those standards? Lateral mobility also seems to characterize professions. From that basic starting point I believe "a professional" might be summarized in the statement that he is one who approaches problems with trained logic, skill and an ability to keep emotions out of business. Now, does law enforcement qualify under all of these descriptions? In my opinion, it is only beginning to in certain communities. One might compare law enforcement as a profession today with public elementary school teaching in the early thirties. Despite obvious differences, I believe the analogy fits.

There are some questions dealing with internal issues that are truly interesting. For example, what kind of a rank structure fits law enforcement best? Does it call for specialization or is a generalist concept better? Does it require special protections as a buffer against politics and fickle budgets? Is union membership compatible with the term professional? What kind of career development services should an individual expect from within his organization? Can anyone and everyone aspire to go all the way to the top, based on job performance and personal qualities? What kind of competitive environment should exist and at what point could internal competition become counter-productive to the organization?

You can appreciate that each of these questions deserves far more exposition than I can give them here, but I want you to know that they define our perspective for looking at means of improving law enforcement. As we look at ourselves, we know that all of the other improvements we have made or contemplate making would be meaningless without some sort of departmental concensus on exactly how professional we want to be and how we intend to get there. We do not have that concensus today, and if we ever get it, it will not come easily because of one of the basic police characteristics that I mentioned at the outset. That is the alienation from some sectors of their own community which tends to drive policemen into a defensive unit that resists outside criticism and change, even when they know the criticism to be valid and that change is needed. The only answer to that barrier lies in communication. This must come gradually, building its strength through a flow of confidence down through the leadership chain so that the climate becomes receptive to change. Of course police have no monopoly on clinging to the status quo. I suggest that you could find it here on this campus and in any of the other professional and business institutions that we have in the city. But transferring concepts is especially difficult in a rumor-driven environment. The facts required to put down rumors and gossip are best conveyed in face-to-face verbal exchanges rather than through written memoranda. My own experience in this respect has ranged from humorous to distinctly uncomfortable and frustrating—but I am learning.

There is also a threshold where resistance mounts in more than straight proportion to the amount of change that one may be trying to institute over a fixed period of time. We are constrained by that very practical consideration. Despite the various obstacles that I have identified in the course of these remarks, I want to leave you with the absolutely positive conviction that we can and will reverse the current success that crime now enjoys here. Much of the answer lies in improving internal professional challenges, opportunity and satisfaction for the many fine officers of our department. They will then lead the head-on attack against criminal elements and traffic abuses that currently disturb our great city.

Thank you for hearing out an amateur in this intensely important area of public concern. I am privileged to have been given the opportunity to serve this city and to be with you this evening.

EVERETT LIBRARY QUEENS COLLEGE
CHARLOTTE, NORTH CAROLINA

DATE DUE

OCT 16 '75			
GAYLORD			PRINTED IN U.S.A.